Our Garden

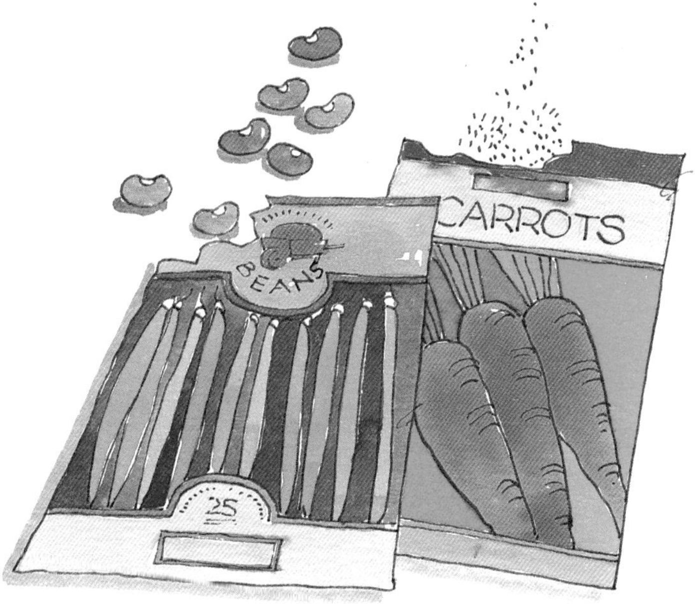

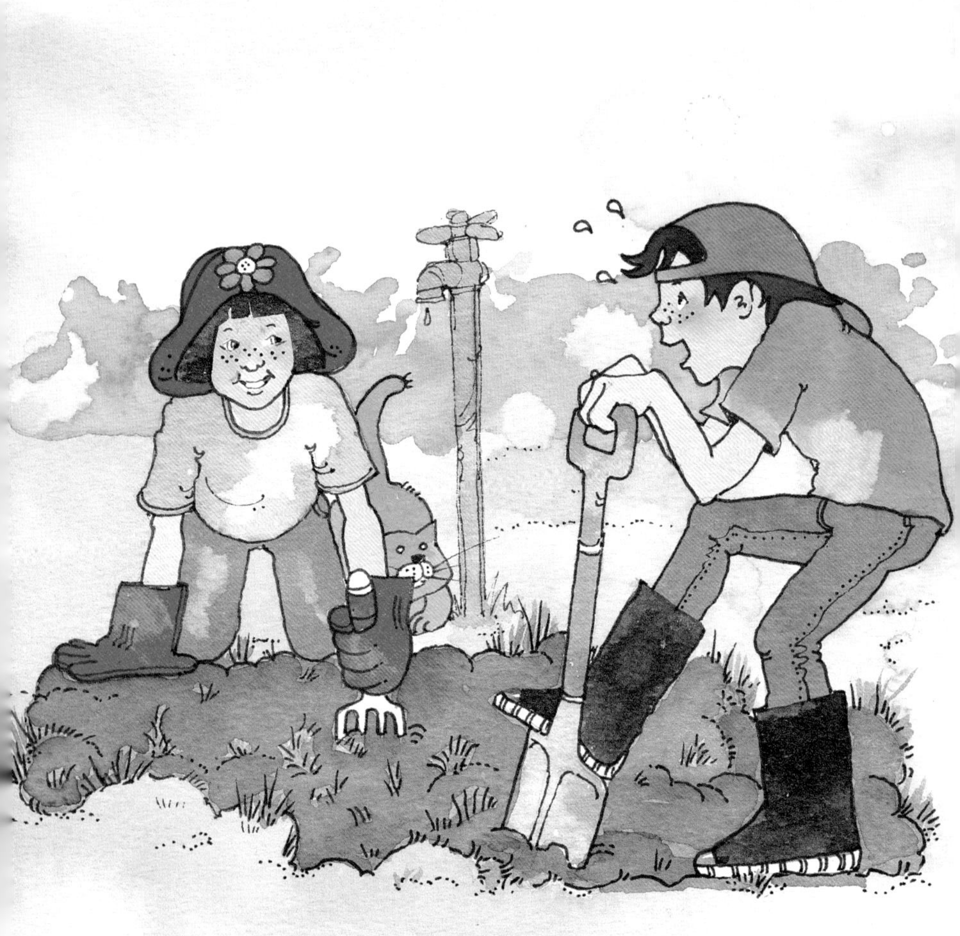

First we dig.

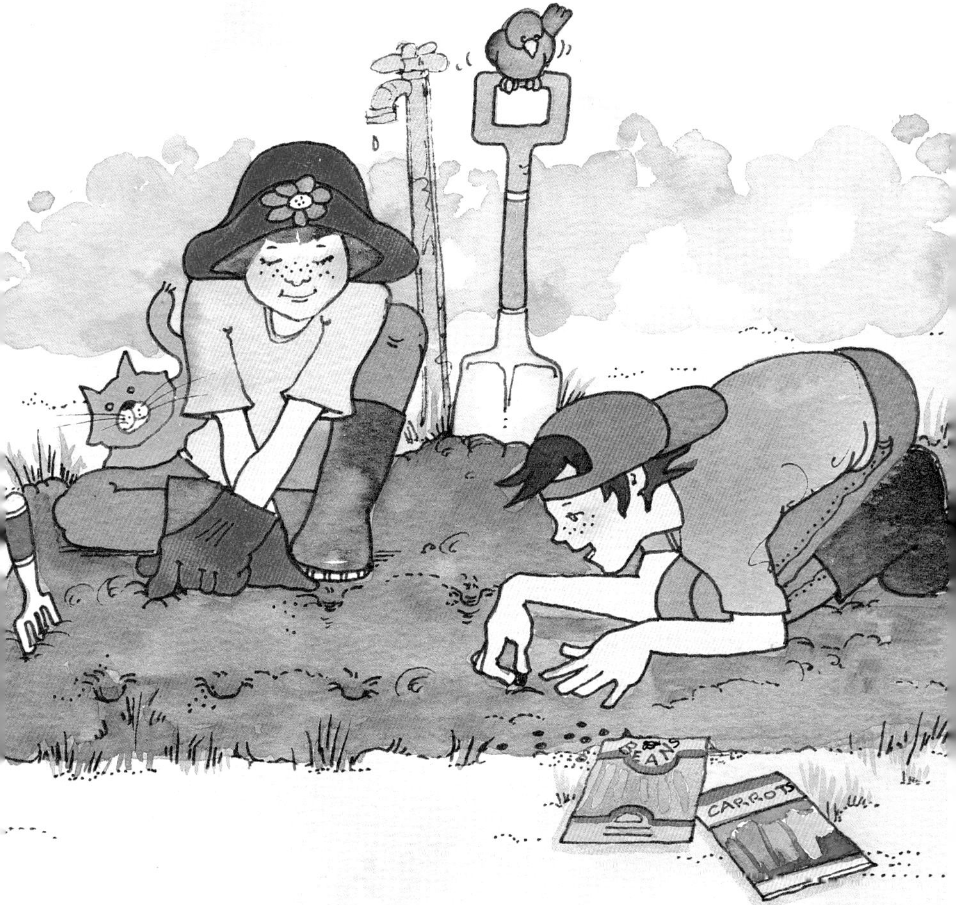

Then we plant.

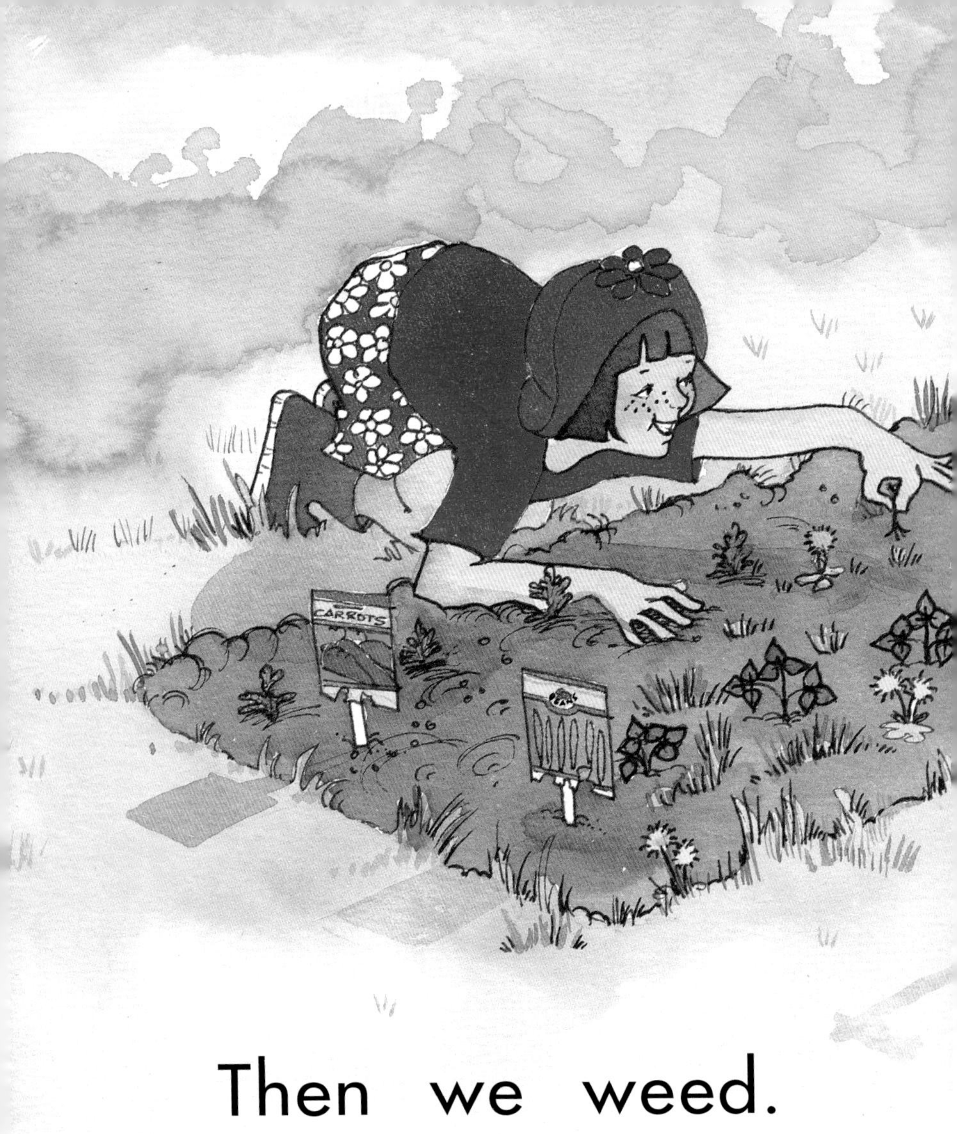

Then we weed.

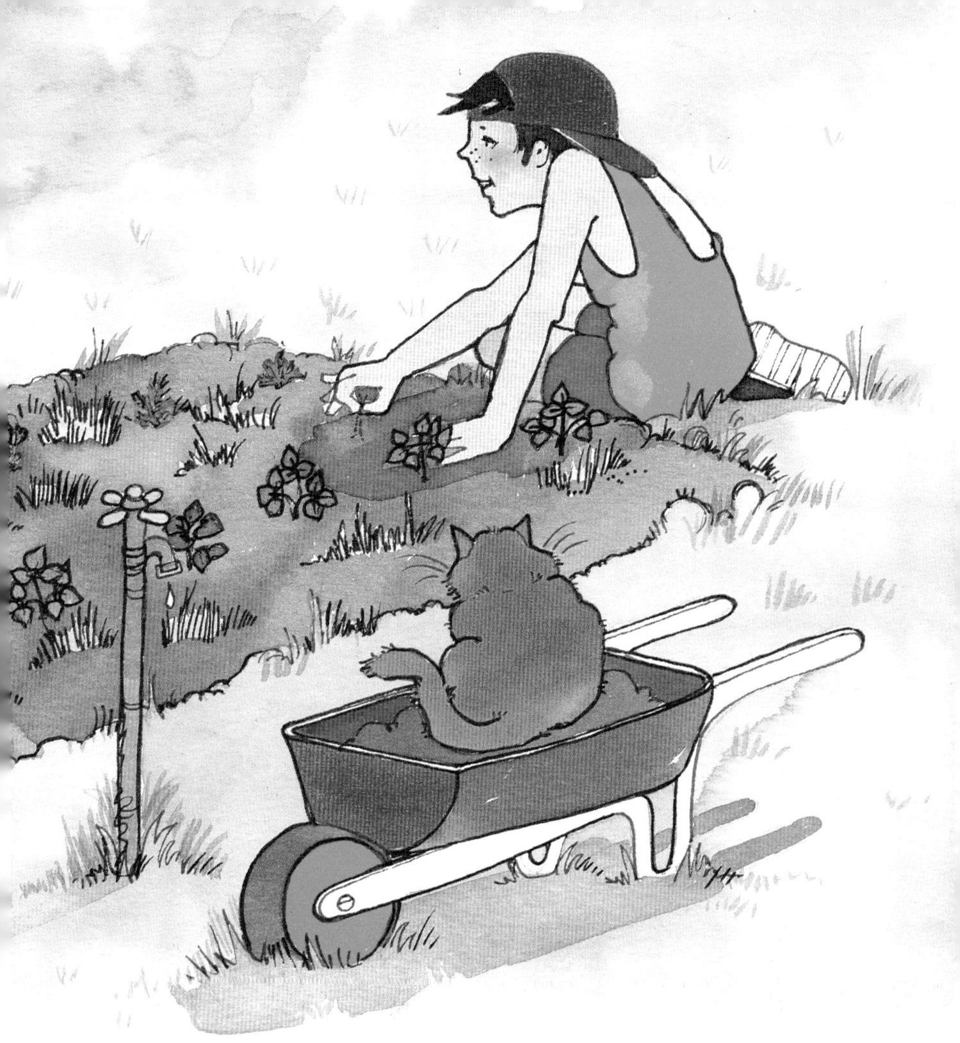

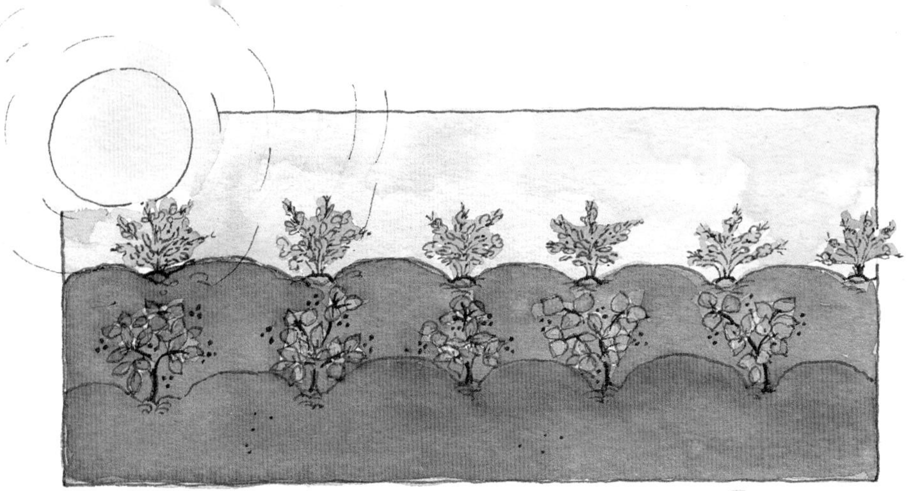

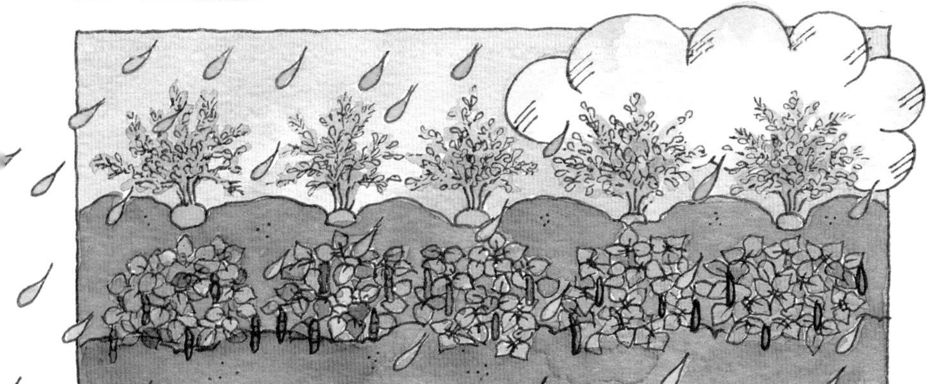

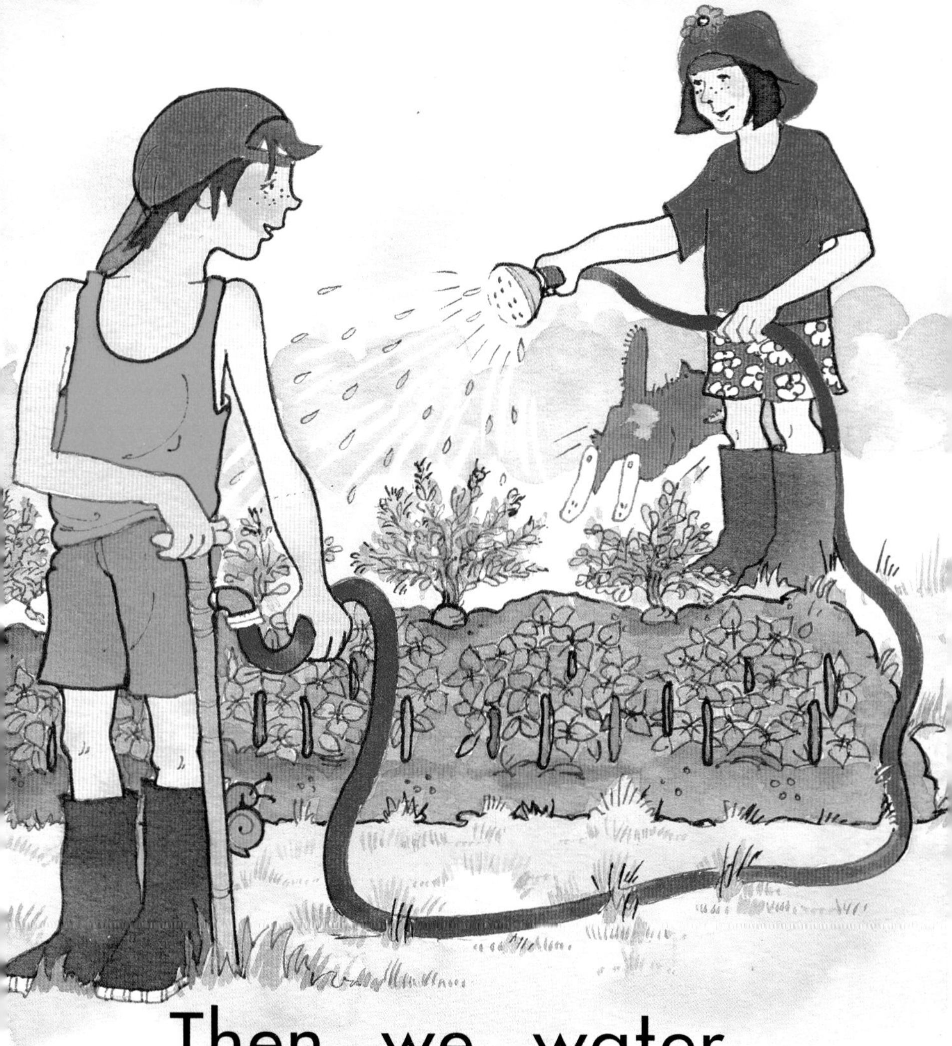

Then we water.

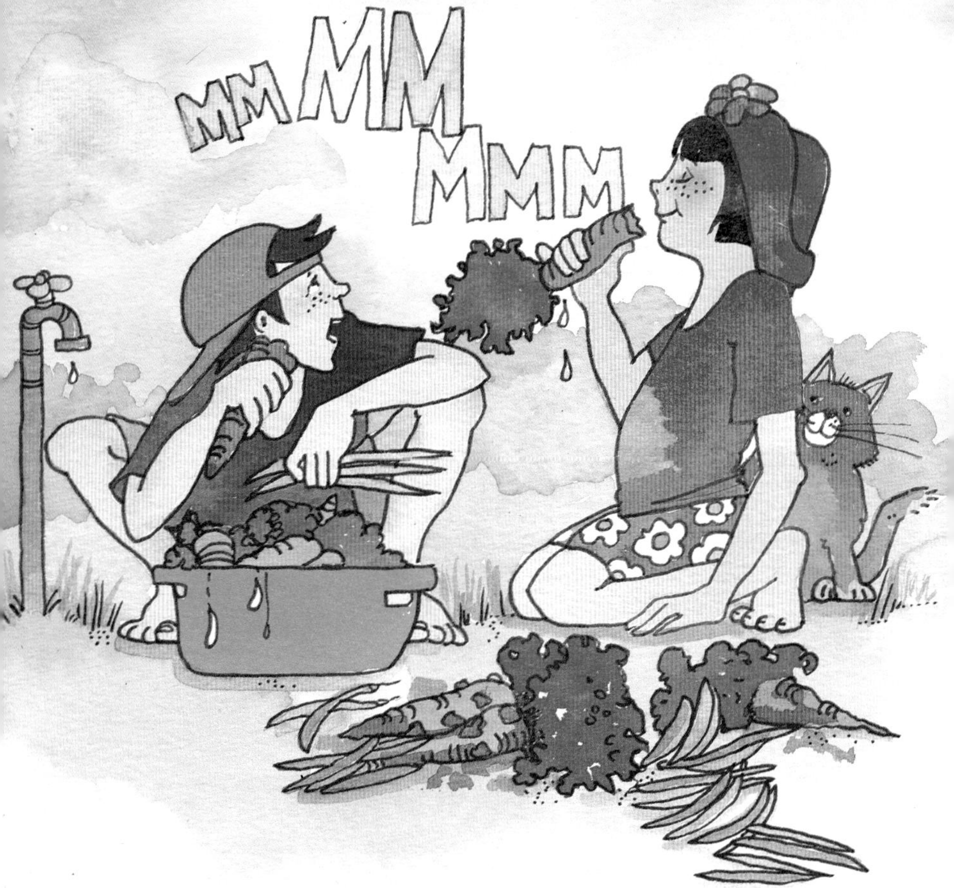

And then we eat!